T0417963

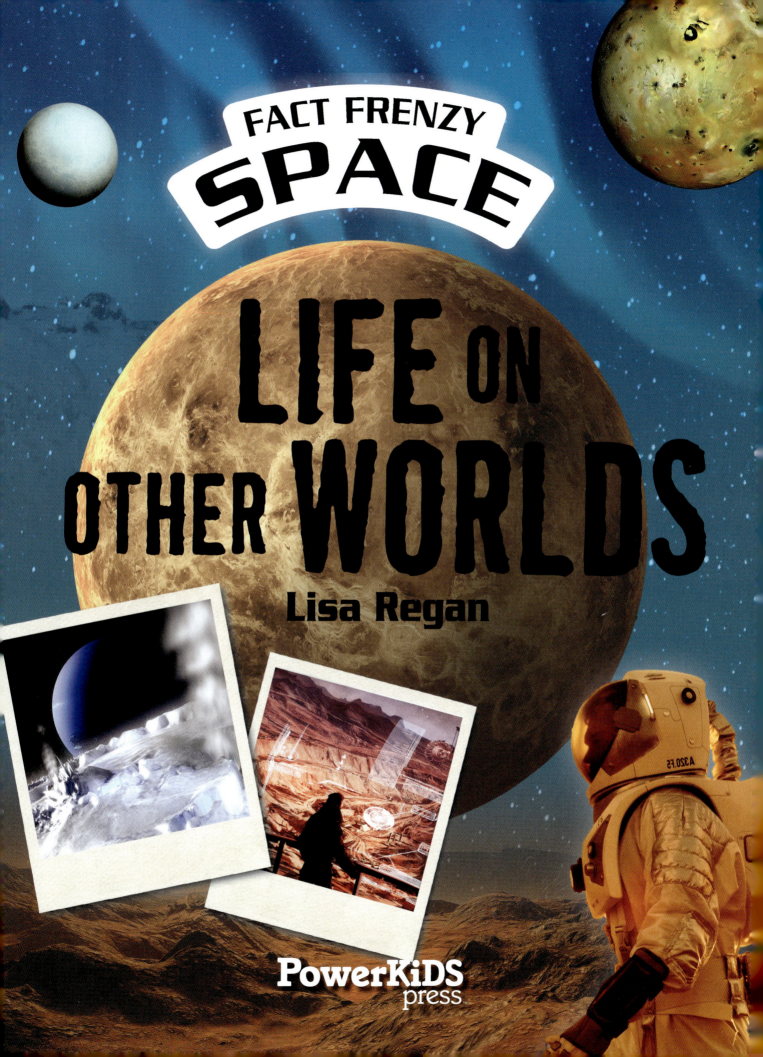

FACT FRENZY
SPACE

LIFE ON OTHER WORLDS

Lisa Regan

PowerKiDS
press

Published in 2021 by
The Rosen Publishing Group, Inc.
29 East 21st Street, New York, NY 10010

Cataloging-in-Publication Data

Names: Regan, Lisa.
Title: Life on other worlds / Lisa Regan.
Description: New York : PowerKids Press, 2021. | Series:
Fact frenzy: space | Includes glossary and index.
Identifiers: ISBN 9781725320208 (pbk.) | ISBN
9781725320222 (library bound) | ISBN 9781725320215
(6 pack)
Subjects: LCSH: Life on other planets--Juvenile literature. |
Exobiology--Juvenile literature. | Life (Biology)--Juvenile
literature.
Classification: LCC QB54.R465 2021 | DDC 576.8'39--dc23

Manufactured in the United States of America

CPSIA Compliance Information: Batch CSPK20: For Further Information contact
Rosen Publishing, New York, New York at 1-800-237-9932.

Find us on

Contents

A DAY IS LONGER THAN A YEAR ON VENUS

A day is how long a planet takes to spin all the way around. A year is how long it takes a planet to circle the sun. A Venus day is 243 Earth days—a year is only 225.

Slow spinner

Venus spins on its axis veeeerry slowly compared with the other planets in our solar system, including Earth. This is why its days are so long. Weirdly, it doesn't always spin around at the same speed. Although it takes around 243 Earth days for Venus to turn all the way around and complete a day, the exact time can vary by up to seven minutes. Scientists are still not entirely sure why.

New day

loading ...

Different days

Venus has the longest day of any planet in our solar system. A day on Mercury—the closest planet to the sun—lasts 59 Earth days, and a day on Mars is just an hour longer than on Earth. Farther out, the other planets are much speedier spinners—a day on Jupiter is just 10 hours, the shortest of all. Saturn (11 hours), Uranus (17 hours), and Neptune (16 hours) aren't too far behind.

Round trip

The closer a planet is to the sun, the shorter its journey around it. Mercury, the closest planet to the sun, completes this loop in just 88 Earth days—giving it the shortest year of all our solar system's planets. A 12-year-old on Earth would be 52 years old if they lived on Mercury! And the longest year? That would be Neptune, where a year is 59,800 Earth days—or just under 164 Earth years.

I'm only six months old on Neptune!

YOU'D WEIGH LESS ON MARS THAN ON EARTH

No, the scale isn't just broken! Your weight is how much matter is in your body—your mass—multiplied by the force of gravity. Mars has less gravity than Earth, so you weigh less there.

> But I wasn't even trying to lose weight!

What is gravity?

Gravity is the force that pulls you down to the ground on Earth so you don't float off into the sky. It is the same force that keeps the moon circling around Earth, and the planets circling around the sun. It's also the force that holds galaxies together. Hmm, yep, gravity plays a pretty important part in the universe!

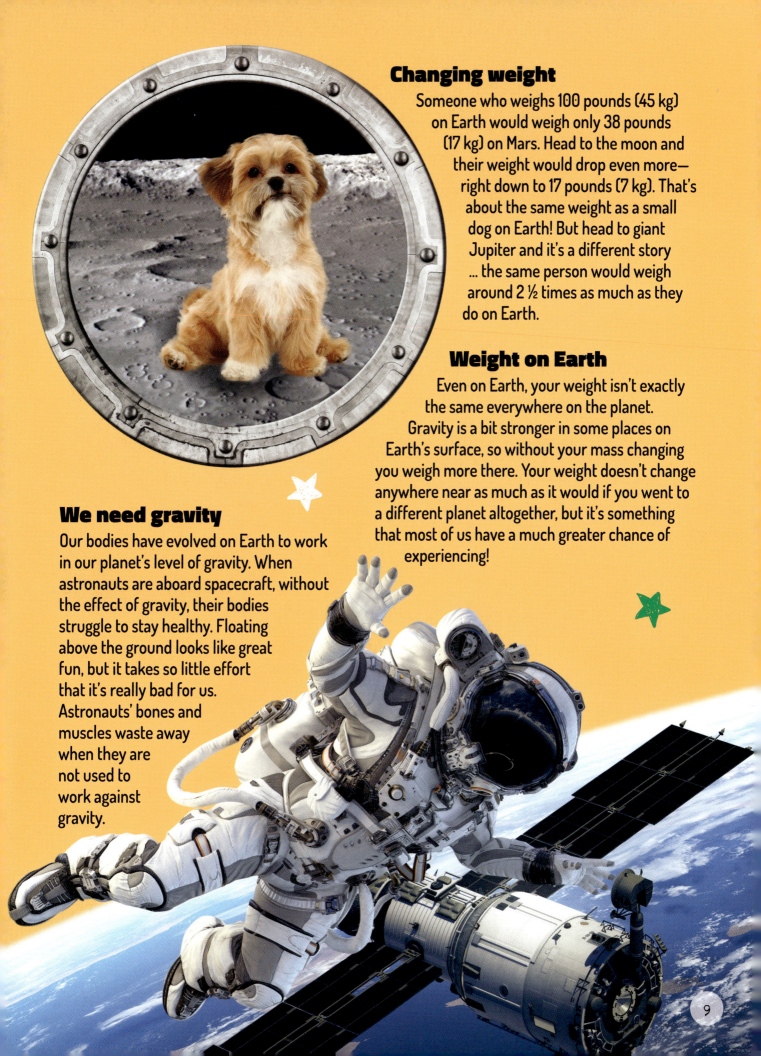

Changing weight

Someone who weighs 100 pounds (45 kg) on Earth would weigh only 38 pounds (17 kg) on Mars. Head to the moon and their weight would drop even more— right down to 17 pounds (7 kg). That's about the same weight as a small dog on Earth! But head to giant Jupiter and it's a different story ... the same person would weigh around 2 ½ times as much as they do on Earth.

Weight on Earth

Even on Earth, your weight isn't exactly the same everywhere on the planet. Gravity is a bit stronger in some places on Earth's surface, so without your mass changing you weigh more there. Your weight doesn't change anywhere near as much as it would if you went to a different planet altogether, but it's something that most of us have a much greater chance of experiencing!

We need gravity

Our bodies have evolved on Earth to work in our planet's level of gravity. When astronauts are aboard spacecraft, without the effect of gravity, their bodies struggle to stay healthy. Floating above the ground looks like great fun, but it takes so little effort that it's really bad for us. Astronauts' bones and muscles waste away when they are not used to work against gravity.

NEPTUNE'S MOON TRITON HAS ICE VOLCANOES

The ice volcanoes shoot out what scientists believe is a mixture of liquid nitrogen, methane, and dust. This instantly freezes and then snows back down to the surface.

> Er, this moon looks a bit cold.

Brrr ... chilly!

It's so incredibly cold on Triton—the surface temperature is -391 °F (-235 °C)—that nitrogen and methane are both usually frozen solid. On Earth, they are usually gases and have to be made very, very cold before they even turn liquid, let alone solid.

FACT 4

It rains liquid methane almost constantly on Titan, Saturn's largest moon.

Pepperoni moon

Io, one of Jupiter's moons, has the most volcanic activity of any object in our solar system. Its surface is covered with hundreds of exploding volcanoes—from far away, it looks a bit like a pepperoni pizza! These volcanoes can shoot jets up to 250 miles (400 km) into the atmosphere, in eruptions so violent that they can be seen by large telescopes on Earth around 391 million miles (630 million km) away.

Not the most appetizing-looking pizza ...

People used to think that the dark patches on the moon were oceans, like those on Earth.

Mercury and the moon

Even when a planet or moon no longer has active volcanoes, scientists can tell from clues on its surface whether it once did. Mercury's and the moon's long-extinct volcanoes have left the remains of their huge lava flows that cooled and turned solid. These show up as dark plains on both their surfaces. The moon also has large bumps on its surface, called lunar domes, which scientists think were made by lava erupting and cooling slowly in that spot.

Volcanoes on Mars

Millions of years ago, Mars used to have the solar system's largest active volcanoes, and the biggest of all was Olympus Mons. Although it is now long dead, it is still visible on Mars's surface. Olympus Mons is over three times the size of Earth's tallest mountain. In fact, it is so large that if you stood at the top you wouldn't even know you were on a mountain. The mountain slopes would stretch to the horizon and then be hidden by the curve of the planet.

FACT 5 — JUPITER AND SATURN MAY HAVE DIAMOND RAIN

Scientists believe that it may rain down diamonds during storms on Jupiter and Saturn. The biggest diamonds would be around 0.4 inch (1 cm) wide—big enough for a nice ring!

How to make diamonds

Do you want to become super rich? Well, first, you should pick up a cow and head to Saturn or Jupiter. Next, wait for a lightning storm. When your cow passes wind, the methane gas will turn into a sooty form of carbon. The soot will fall back down through the planet's deep atmosphere. As it goes, it will be crushed into diamonds, which are just another form of carbon. Ta-da!

FACT 6

Beyond our solar system, there is a planet twice the size of Earth that scientists think may be almost entirely made of diamond.

Is space the future of diamond mining?

Diamond seas

Scientists think that once these solid diamonds are formed, they move farther into the planet and eventually become liquid. This would create a liquid sea around the planet's core. Saturn and Jupiter are both gas giants, so their composition is very different from Earth. They look solid from far away, but they are mostly made of squashed gases around a small solid or liquid core.

Space mining

Precious gems are big business on Earth—and, in the future, maybe even beyond Earth! The idea is that spacecraft could travel to other planets in our solar system, carrying robot mining ships that are able to collect the diamonds there. The spacecraft would then bring them back to Earth, to make some genuinely out-of-this-world jewels!

Odd weather

In the last 25 years or so, scientists have started exploring all the weird and wonderful planets outside our solar system. These are called exoplanets—and boy, do they have some strange weather of their own! On one planet, it snows rocks. On another, it rains burning-hot glass sideways—you wouldn't want to get caught out in that, even with an umbrella. Yikes!

SATURN'S RINGS SOMETIMES DISAPPEAR

Around every 15 years, a trick of the sunlight makes it look to us as if Saturn's rings have vanished! The last time this happened was in 2009—keep your eyes out for next time!

Thin rings

Saturn's rings are enormous, big enough to stretch around a planet 764 times bigger than Earth. But they are also very thin—scientists think that in some places they are just 30 feet (10 m) wide. Even at their thickest point, the rings are only 0.6 mile (1 km) across, which an average person could walk in around 10 minutes.

FACT 8

One of Saturn's moons has a ridge around the middle, making it look like a giant walnut shell. Scientists think it formed when the moon absorbed some of Saturn's rings.

But I like my rings, I don't want them to disappear!

14

Disappearing trick

As Saturn moves around the sun, it sometimes turns its rings edge-on to Earth. The rings are so thin that in a small telescope it looks like they've disappeared altogether! Around 400 years ago, this sight puzzled Galileo, one of the greatest space scientists of all time. Having first spotted the rings in 1610, he was very confused when they seemed to vanish again within two years. For a short time, he even stopped studying Saturn!

But ... the rings were right there! Weren't they?

Closer look

Saturn's rings are a wonderful sight, but do you know what they're made of? Dust, rock, and ice. Hmm, not quite as glamorous as they seem from a distance. The pieces that make up the rings vary in size, from a grain of sand to a large-ish house. The rings speed around and around Saturn at great speed. It looks like Saturn has seven rings, but each of these is split up into smaller rings—called ringlets.

Neptune and its rings

Not so special

Saturn is not the only planet in our solar system to have rings surrounding it. In fact, all the other giant planets in our solar system—Jupiter, Uranus, and Neptune—have similar rings. Saturn's are famous for being the biggest and by far the most impressive sight, though. The other planets' rings are much darker and cannot easily be seen from Earth.

FACT 9

THE MOON IS FALLING TOWARD US!

The moon has been free-falling toward the Earth for billions of years. But don't panic! It is being pulled sideways at the same time, so it doesn't actually get closer to Earth.

Earth's gravity

What keeps you on Earth's surface instead of floating through the sky and out into space? That's right, it's gravity. Earth's gravity constantly pulls you toward its middle—and you and the moon have that in common! It is the reason that the moon circles around and around Earth, rather than whizzing off into space.

Sideways pull

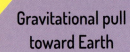

Aaarrrrghhh, I'm falling!

Gravitational pull toward Earth

We've been over this, you're always falling ...

At high speed

If you drop a ball from your hand, it will fall straight down to the ground. But if you throw a ball hard straight ahead of you, and there is nothing in the way, it will travel through the air for a while and then fall downward until it eventually lands on the ground. The moon is moving at high speed around Earth, so the downward pull of gravity isn't the only force acting on it.

Falling around Earth

Now imagine if you could throw the ball really fast. It would take a long time to drop down to Earth. If you could throw it superhumanly fast, it would never fall to the ground but just keep moving around and around Earth. This is what the moon is doing! It is far enough away, and moves fast enough, that it never crashes down to Earth's surface, but instead constantly falls in a curve around Earth.

Balancing act

If the moon moved a lot faster than it does, it would break away entirely from the pull of Earth's gravity and fly off into space. If it moved much slower, it would be dragged all the way down by Earth's gravity and crash into our planet. The perfect balance between the moon's speed and its gravity means that it stays in constant orbit around Earth.

When rockets are launched into space, their speed is set to either join or escape Earth's orbit.

SUNSETS ON MARS ARE BLUE

On Earth, we are used to blue sky in the day and red-orange sunsets in the evening. On Mars, it's the other way around! It has a red sky in the day, with blue sunsets.

YOU CAN SEE MARS IN THE NIGHT SKY WITHOUT A TELESCOPE FOR MOST OF THE YEAR.

Blue skies

On Earth, the particles that make up our atmosphere—the layers of gases that surround our planet—partly block the sun's light and scatter it around the sky. They are much better at scattering blue light than red light, so we see this blue light spread across the sky. This means that most of the time on Earth our sky looks blue.

Look, the sun's going down. Must be quitting time!

Reddish sunset

At sunset, Earth's position has moved so that the sun is now on the horizon rather than appearing high in the sky. The sun's light now has to pass through so much of Earth's atmosphere that all the blue light is scattered away so that other shades can be seen. This is why sunsets on Earth have their beautiful golden-reddish-orange glow.

Yeah, yeah, the orange is pretty, but I prefer black and white!

Reddish skies

On Mars, things are a little different. Mars has lots and lots of dust in its atmosphere, which blocks all shades of light about the same amount. This dust is reddish, which makes it absorb the blue light and scatter the red light, so on Mars the sky is usually red.

Blue sunset

The reason that Mars has blue sunsets has to do with these dust particles, too. Looking at the sun from Mars, there is actually always a blue halo around it, but it is only when the sun appears on the horizon that its light passes through all the dust and the blue halo is easy to see.

IF YOU PUT SATURN IN A GIANT BATH, IT WOULD FLOAT

You'd need to find a bathtub 38,000 miles (60,000 km) wide to give this a try, but it's true—Saturn is so light for its size that it would float on the surface of water.

I am just so relaxed right now!

SATURN IS A SLIGHTLY SQUISHED CIRCLE SHAPE, WIDEST AROUND ITS MIDDLE.

Huge but light

Saturn is huge, big enough to fit 764 Earths inside it. But although it takes up so much space, the lightness of the materials that make it up means that it doesn't have very much mass for its size at all. Another way to say this is that it has low density. Because it has a lower density than liquid water, Saturn should float on the surface of water, just like a beach ball or a boat does.

Gassy giant

What makes Saturn so light, when it's so huge? In a word, gas. Saturn is a different sort of planet than Earth—while Earth is made of relatively heavy solids and liquids, Saturn is mostly made of gases, which are much lighter. In fact, Saturn's main gases are especially light ones—hydrogen and helium, the lightest elements in existence (as far as we know).

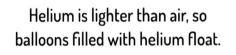

Helium is lighter than air, so balloons filled with helium float.

The Cassini spacecraft exploring Saturn and its moons.

Mysterious middle

Scientists think Saturn has either a liquid or a solid core in its middle, but they're still not sure exactly which it is. Saturn is a long way from Earth—at its closest to us, it is still 746 million miles (1.2 billion km) away. That's over 3,000 times farther away than the moon! A spacecraft called Cassini spent over 10 years exploring around Saturn, but there's still a lot for us to learn about the planet.

Tricky test

Can you imagine trying to float a giant, swirling ball of gas in a bathtub almost 1,000 times bigger than Earth? It's pretty tricky without a solid surface because we can't even know for sure where Saturn starts and finishes! Well, "floating Saturn" shows us the very real truth that it's less dense than liquid water—but, in reality, it probably wouldn't work quite as well as a nice rubber duck!

BILLIONS OF PLANETS DON'T CIRCLE ANY STAR

"Rogue planets" are free-floating planets that have broken away from a star and wander through the universe. They're the rebel runaways of the planet world!

I'm a rebel without a star!

Breaking free

When new solar systems are forming, it's absolute chaos. All sorts of materials swirl around a star in a packed, top-speed confusion, whizzing past and crashing into each other as they go. Most scientists believe that at these times many planets are thrown out of the mix with such force that they leave the system altogether and speed off alone through space.

Violent crashes may send rogue planets spinning off alone into space.

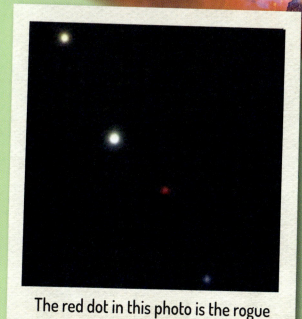

The red dot in this photo is the rogue planet PSO J318.5–22.

Giant runaways

Rogue planets are big. Waaay bigger than Earth. In fact, the smallest rogue planets are around the size of Jupiter—which is our solar system's largest planet by far, big enough to fit 1,300 Earths inside it. There aren't just the odd few of them wandering around space, either—scientists think there may be twice as many rogue planets as there are stars in the universe!

Tricky to spot

Despite their huge size, rogue planets are actually very hard for scientists to spot. They do not give off any light, and as they aren't near a star, they can't be seen interfering with the light it gives off—which is how scientists can see many star-circling planets. When rogue planets pass in front of far-off stars, scientists can see the effect of this and work out that they are there, but it is very rare.

Rogue life?

Hello!

We get our light and heat from the sun, our nearest star. But rogue planets don't have a friendly nearby star to keep them nice and toasty warm, so they are very cold. Not quite as cold as you may think, though. Rogue planets produce some heat of their own, maybe even enough to support life—although of a very different kind to anything on Earth ...

JUPITER HAS A STORM BIGGER THAN EARTH

Jupiter's Great Red Spot is a huge, swirling storm that can easily be seen on the planet's surface. It has been going on for 350 years and Earth could fit inside it with room to spare.

Supersized

Jupiter is the biggest planet in our solar system by a lot—all our solar system's other planets could fit inside it with room to spare! And scientists think this supersized planet's equally supersized storm has been raging since more than 100 years before the United States was founded! Earth's longest recorded storm, Hurricane John, back in 1994, lasted just 31 days.

A storm the size of Earth is "little?!"

Neptune's Great Dark Spot

Shrinking storm

Jupiter's Great Red Spot has shrunk to half the size it was when it was first seen. It looks like it's finally dying down after all this time, and scientists think that in 20 years' time we probably won't be able to see it from Earth at all. The thick clouds around Jupiter don't help, as they make it quite hard to see the planet's surface.

Other Great Spots

Neptune and Saturn also have their own "Great Spots," whirling storms that can be seen from Earth. They aren't as reliable as Jupiter's Great Red Spot, though—they seem to disappear and they sometimes appear again in other places on the planet. Saturn has different Great White Spots and Neptune has a Great Dark Spot, but only about half the time.

The Little Red Spot

Jupiter has lots of storms whirling around all over its surface. The Little Red Spot is another storm on Jupiter that has been growing since it was first spotted in 2006. It formed when three smaller storms joined together, and it is now around the same size as Earth. So not that little after all!

Imagine if Earth's storms joined together.

EVEN MORE FACTS!

You've found out lots about life on other worlds, but there's always more to discover! Boost your knowledge here with even more facts.

Daytime temperatures on Mercury, the closest planet to the sun, can reach over 801°F (427°C). At night, with no atmosphere to keep the daytime heat, temperatures plummet to –290°F (–180°C).

Mars is named after the Roman god of war. The ancient Greeks called the planet "Ares," after their god of war. The ancient Egyptians called Mars "Har decher," meaning "the red one."

NASA has sent four robotic vehicles, called rovers, to explore the surface of Mars. In 2021, a fifth rover, called Mars 2020, is being planned. It will look for signs of past or present life, and see if humans could one day explore Mars.

Venus is named after the Roman goddess of love. It's the brightest object in the night sky apart from the moon. It can be seen so easily without a telescope that some ancient civilizations thought it was two stars, a morning star and an evening star.

Between 1995 and 2003, the Galileo spacecraft orbited and studied Jupiter and its moons, sending back images of gigantic lava flows; lava lakes; and towering, collapsing mountains.

Jupiter has 79 moons that we know about. The four moons Ganymede, Io, Europa, and Callisto are called the Galilean moons, because they were first discovered by the Italian astronomer Galileo Galilei, in 1610.

Saturn is named after the Roman god of agriculture. It has 53 moons, and nine more that we need to learn more about. Four spacecraft have visited Saturn, including Pioneer 11, Cassini, and Voyager 1 and 2.

Uranus is the seventh planet from the sun and Neptune's neighbor. It spins lying on its side, which means on parts of Uranus it is light for up to 42 years and then dark for 42 years.

Neptune is the most distant planet from the sun. It's an ice giant, made of water, ammonia, and methane over a solid center. The methane gives Neptune a blue color.

Pluto is a dwarf planet 3-5 billion miles from the sun. A person standing on Pluto would weigh about one-fifteenth of what they weigh on Earth.

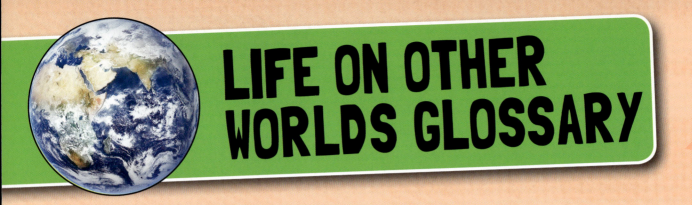

LIFE ON OTHER WORLDS GLOSSARY

ammonia A colorless gas or liquid with a strong, sharp smell.

astronaut A person trained for traveling in a spacecraft.

astronomer A scientist who studies the stars, planets, and other natural objects in space.

atmosphere A shell of gases kept around a planet, star, or other object by its gravity.

axis An imaginary line through the middle of something.

carbon A chemical element that occurs in carbon dioxide, coal, and oil.

core The central part of an object.

density A measure of the compactness of a substance or object, expressed as the relation of its mass to its volume.

dwarf planet A world, orbiting a star, that looks like a planet but does not meet certain criteria needed to make it a true planet.

Earth day The length of time (24 hours) it takes Earth to make one complete rotation on its axis.

exoplanet A planet orbiting a star outside our solar system.

free-falling Descending with only the force of gravity acting against the movement.

galaxy A large system of stars, gas, and dust with anything from millions to trillions of stars.

gems Valuable stones used in jewelry.

gravity A natural force created around objects with mass, which draws other objects toward them.

helium A colorless, very light gas that has no smell, and has the lowest known boiling point.

hydrogen A colorless gas that is the lightest and most common element in the universe.

lava Very hot, liquid rock that comes out of volcano.

mass The amount of physical matter in an object

methane A colorless gas that has no smell. Natural gas consists mostly of methane.

moon Earth's closest companion in space, a ball of rock that orbits Earth every 27.3 days. Most other planets in the solar system have moons of their own.

NASA An abbreviation for "National Aeronautics and Space Administration," the American government organization concerned with spacecraft and space travel.

nitrogen A colorless gas that has no smell. Nitrogen makes up the biggest portion of Earth's atmosphere.

orbit A fixed path taken by one object in space around another because of the effect of gravity.

planet A world, orbiting a star, which has enough mass and gravity to pull itself into a ball-like shape, and clear space around it of other large objects.

rogue planet A planet that has broken off from a star, or formed on its own, and free-floats in space without orbiting a star.

rover A small, remote-controlled vehicle that roams over planets in space, taking photographs and gathering rock and soil samples.

solar system The eight planets (including Earth) and their moons, and other objects such as asteroids, that orbit around the sun.

spacecraft A vehicle that travels into space.

telescope A device that collects light or other radiations from space and uses them to create a bright, clear image. Telescopes can use either a lens or a mirror to collect light.

universe The whole of space including all the galaxies, solar systems, stars, and planets.

volcano A mountain from which hot, melted rock, gas, steam, and ash sometimes burst.

FURTHER INFORMATION

BOOKS

Aguilar, David. *Space Encyclopedia*. London, UK: National Geographic Kids, 2013.

Becklade, Sue. *Wild About Space*. Thaxted, UK: Miles Kelly, 2020.

Betts, Bruce. *Astronomy for Kids: How to Explore Outer Space with Binoculars, a Telescope, or Just Your Eyes!* Emeryville, CA: Rockridge Press, 2018.

DK. *The Astronomy Book: Big Ideas Simply Explained*. London, UK: DK, 2017.

DK. *Knowledge Encyclopedia Space!: The Universe As You've Never Seen It Before*. London, UK: DK, 2015.

Frith, Alex, Jerome Martin, and Alice James. *100 Things to Know About Space*. London, UK: Usborne Publishing, 2016.

National Geographic Kids. *Everything: Space*. London, UK: Collins, 2018.

WEBSITES

Ducksters Astronomy for Kids
http://www.ducksters.com/science/astronomy.php
Head to this website to find out all there is to know about astronomy; you can also try an astronomy crossword puzzle and word search!

NASA Science: Space Place
https://spaceplace.nasa.gov
Discover all sorts of facts about space, other planets, and the moon. You can even play the Mars Rover Game, sending commands to the Mars rover and collecting as much data as possible in eight expeditions!

Science Kids: Space for Kids
http://www.sciencekids.co.nz/space.html
Go beyond our planet and explore space through fun facts, games, videos, quizzes and projects.

Publisher's note to educators and parents: Our editors have carefully reviewed these websites to ensure that they are suitable for students. Many websites change frequently, however, and we cannot guarantee that a site's future contents will continue to meet our high standards of quality and educational value. Be advised that students should be closely supervised whenever they access the Internet.

INDEX

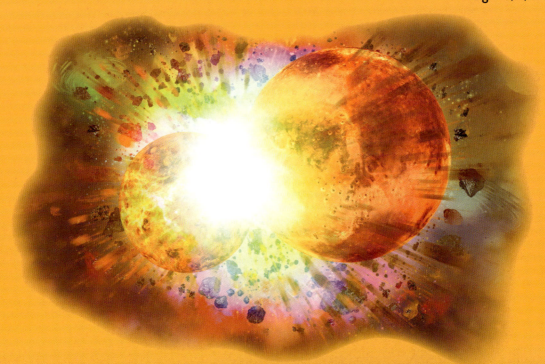